How to find out

A guide to information sc

Claire Drinkwater and Gwyneth Price

Newsam Library, Institute of Education, University of London

First published in 2003 by
Librarians of Institutes and Schools of Education

© Librarians of Institutes and Schools of Education

British Library Cataloguing in Publication Data:
A catalogue record for this publication is available from the British Library

ISBN 0-901922-37-4

Production Services by
Book Production Consultants plc, Cambridge
Printed by Wrightson

Contents

Acknowledgements   v

Chapter 1   Introduction   1
             What this book covers; how to use it

Chapter 2   The education system in the UK   4
             General information on the education system and the
             National Curriculum

Chapter 3   The qualifications maze   10
             School examinations and examination boards; degrees
             and vocational qualifications; international equivalence

Chapter 4   Choosing a school or university   16
             Listings of schools; performance tables and inspection
             reports; guides to courses in further and higher education;
             review reports

Chapter 5   The legal framework   22
             Legislation and government reports; guidance and
             interpretation of the law

Chapter 6   Equal opportunities and inclusive education   28
             Legislation relating to equal opportunities in education;
             disability and special needs education

Chapter 7   Statistics   34
             Finding national and international statistics

Chapter 8	**What's new?**	40
	News stories, current and past; press releases; coming events	
Chapter 9	**History of education**	44
	Chronologies; general histories; biographical sources; finding source material	
Chapter 10	**The international perspective**	49
	Education systems; international schools and colleges; working and studying abroad	
Bibliography		55

Acknowledgements

We should like to thank all our colleagues in LISE and at the Newsam Library, Institute of Education, for their assistance and encouragement in the production of this book. In particular, we are indebted to Diana Guthrie, Alan Bradwell, John Makin, Roy Kirk and Alison Harding for their help in reading the draft versions and suggesting additional materials; and to Gill Sims and Andrew Page for their constant encouragement.

This book has been a joint effort throughout, and would never have been completed without the mutual support provided by working together. Finally, we both wish to acknowledge our debt to the late Michael Humby, former Head of Reader Services at the Institute of Education Library and our mentor in reference work in education.

Claire Drinkwater
Gwyneth Price

1 *Introduction*

Education affects all of us in one way or another – as school child or parent, teacher or student, school governor or researcher – or as a librarian trying to help all these people find the information they need. As pressure builds in the political agenda, so education becomes more complex and more liable to change, with new legislation, new curriculum guidelines, new systems of examinations and, in times of ever increasing mobility, a growing international dimension as well. This book is intended to be a starting point for enquirers. It aims to provide an accessible introduction to the wealth of information sources available in this increasingly complex subject.

We hope that the book will prove useful to a wide range of people. Students and researchers new to the field will find it a handy overview of the range of sources available to them. Parents and governors might use it as a guide to finding specific information that they require. For librarians, we hope it will provide an introduction and a useful tool both for those dealing with education queries in a general enquiry service, and for new recruits in an education library.

Arrangement

Our starting point in compiling the book was the questions people ask. Experience at the enquiry desk in a major education library has shown us that some questions come up again and again, and can often be answered from more than one source. We have therefore arranged the book by topic, and provided a sample of questions at the head of each chapter to illustrate the area it covers. We have deliberately avoided the formal arrangement of sources according to format, preferring to concentrate on their usefulness for a particular type of query.

One problem in writing a book of this kind is providing full information without choking the text with excessive detail. We have tried to overcome this by dividing the book into two main sections. Chapters 2–10 are intended to provide a readable introduction to each topic. Within the text, information about sources is kept to a minimum, often only a title. Full details of both books and websites are listed at the end of each chapter. The bibliography section brings together all these references, and provides a complete list of the information sources we have used. Librarians might like to use this as a checklist or guide to basic sources in building up a reference collection in education.

Selection of sources

This is not by any means a comprehensive list of information sources in education. Our aim has never been to survey all such works currently available. Instead, we have tried to select for each chapter those we have found most useful in answering the questions. Factors such as accessibility, coverage, currency and ease of use have consciously influenced our choice, though no doubt personal preferences and prejudices have crept in from time to time.

Our base is in London, and this has inevitably affected the scope of the book. Education across the UK is becoming more varied, as devolution leads to more independent decision making in Wales and Northern Ireland, as well as in Scotland. We have set out to deal thoroughly with sources for education in England, and wherever possible to include also information for the similar, but now diverging, education system of Wales. Education in Scotland has always differed substantially from that south of the border and, although we have included references to one or two important information sources, we have not tried to cover the Scottish system in any detail. Northern Ireland has remained almost entirely outside our remit.

Books and websites

We have included both printed and electronic sources in each chapter. Traditionally, the kind of queries we are looking at here would have been answered from a range of reference books such as directories and encyclopedias, and these are still essential sources. Many people will find them easier to use, and more readily accessible than their electronic counterparts. But no modern enquiry service could operate without access to the internet and the opportunities for fuller and more up-to-date information which it offers. Of course, websites are only as accurate as the people who provide them, and they too can be out of date, as well as having an irritating habit of moving address or disappearing altogether. We have tried to ensure that all the information provided in this book is accurate at time of going to press, but we recognise that inevitably some of it will be out of date almost at once.

Finally, there are two things that this book does not set out to do. It is not a guide to the research literature or to literature searching. It contains few, if any, references to journal articles or conference papers or how to find them. For an introduction to this aspect of the study of education, we recommend *Researching Education* by Bob Smeaton.[1] Nor do we aim, either in this book, or in the sources it lists, to provide anything more than information. For expert advice, enquirers will need to contact other agencies, such as Citizens Advice Bureaux, trade unions or specialist advice agencies.

Reference

1. Smeaton R.F. (1999), *Researching Education: Reference tools and networks*. London: Librarians of Institutes and Schools of Education.

2 The education system in the UK

> *Key questions:*
> *At what age do children start school in England? What types of secondary school are there? Do private schools cover the same subjects? What is the National Curriculum? What ages do the key stages cover?*

Apparently simple questions are sometimes the hardest to answer. We all know how the education system works – or do we? Our first-hand experience is probably both limited and dated. In this chapter we look at the broad outline of the education system; sources for more detailed information on various aspects of education are covered in later sections.

Making sure that information is current is a problem for enquirers in any subject area, and education is no exception. In recent years a series of Education Acts has brought about major changes to the education system of the UK, making it especially important that the sources used to answer questions concerning it are up to date. Online sources such as websites appear to be the most obvious choices to avoid this problem, but there is no guarantee that information offered online is current: it is always worth checking when it was last updated.

Another complication is provided by the differences between regions in the UK. Scotland's education system has always been substantially different from England's, and devolution has lead to a wider divergence between Wales and England as well.

General sources

Among print sources, annual publications are the most likely to be current. *Whitaker's Almanack*,[1] for instance, contains a brief outline of the education system in the UK, and some basic statistics. Dictionaries and handbooks are also likely to contain useful summaries, but may not be so recent. Lawton and Gordon's *Dictionary of Education*[2] includes a three-page outline of the education system, as well as brief essays discussing key concepts in education, but was published in 1996. The *Blackwell Handbook of Education*[3] also offers alphabetical entries for key terms, but no general overview, and has not been updated since 1995.

For a fuller account, a recent book designed as an introduction to the structure and organisation of the UK education system is Gearon's *Education in the United Kingdom*.[4] This includes chapters on various aspects of the system, and looks in some detail at recent developments and changes. Another printed account is provided by *Education in England, Wales and Northern Ireland: A guide to the system*,[5] published in 1999. An updated version (2002) is available online on the Eurydice website,[6] which also contains useful comparative material on other European countries. Other sources useful for international comparisons include the *International Encyclopedia of Education* (1994)[7] and the *International Encyclopedia of National Systems of Education* (1995).[8] Both are based on the same data and contain outlines in a standard format for each country. An updated edition is available in CD-ROM format as *Education: The complete encyclopedia* (1998).[9]

Websites

Among websites the *Teachernet* website, developed by the Department for Education and Skills (DfES) as a resource for people working in schools, contains a good overview, under the heading *UK education system*.[10] It covers system structure, with separate sections on England and Wales, Scotland and Northern Ireland, examinations and qualifications, and government organisations, and provides a glossary of acronyms and key terms. Each page gives the date when last updated, so it is always possible to see how current the information is. This website also contains other useful sections on government strategy for education, areas currently under discussion and links to other sites, including international sources for comparison.

The British Council website[11] also includes a good summary of the UK education system on its education pages. It covers school education, further education and higher education. Under school education, for instance, it looks at funding and management, structure and curriculum, examinations and assessment, and quality assurance, clearly showing the differences between the constituent countries of the UK. Further details about the distinctive features of the Scottish education system can be found on the British Council's *Education UK Scotland* site.[12]

Another good overview of the whole system is provided on the *BBC News* website, under *Education: UK systems*.[13] This includes a description of the system, emphasising recent changes and developments, alongside current news items on education.

Historical context

Not all questions demand purely current information. For those wishing to see the education system in a historical and political context, *The Education System Transformed* by Clyde Chitty[14] provides an excellent account from 1944 up to the date of publication in 1999, with particular emphasis on recent developments. *Education in the UK: Facts and figures*[15] also sets the current system in its historical context, with details of the legislation and official reports that have transformed the system over recent years, as well as substantial sections on systems and processes.

Curriculum initiatives

Information about the National Curriculum is often in demand. The latest version of the National Curriculum is published as *The National Curriculum for England: Handbook for primary teachers in England*,[16] covering key stages 1 and 2, and *The National Curriculum for England: Handbook for secondary teachers in England*,[17] covering key stages 3 and 4. Separate booklets are also available for individual subjects, covering all the key stages at which they are included in the compulsory curriculum. *National Curriculum online*[18] is the corresponding website. Besides details of the curriculum itself, it also includes schemes of work, support materials and links to other websites and teaching resources.

Details of the Welsh National Curriculum, now administered separately, are available on the website of the Qualifications, Curriculum and Assessment Authority for Wales (ACCAC).[19] In Scotland, the curriculum is less prescriptive than elsewhere in the UK. Guidelines for the 5–14 curriculum are published on the website of Learning and Teaching Scotland.[20]

Good detailed summaries of the National Curriculum and its key stages can also be found in some reference books. *Running a School: Legal duties and responsibilities*[21] aims to provide essential information for headteachers and administrators, and covers the topic from their point of view. *Education in the UK: Facts and figures*[15] also contains a good basic account.

More recent curriculum initiatives include the National Literacy Strategy and the National Numeracy Strategy. Both are available as printed documents: *National Literacy Strategy: Framework for teaching*[22] appeared in its third edition in 2001, and *The National Numeracy Strategy: Framework for teaching mathematics*[23] was published in 1999. The DfES also publish these documents and many later reports and support materials on *The standards site* section of their website.[24]

Higher education and teacher education

Higher education is another area likely to attract queries, especially from potential students. For detailed information on choosing a university, see Chapter 4. International students seeking more general information about the system, including costs and equivalent qualifications, will find much useful information on the British Council's *Education UK* website,[11] which provides a course-search facility, as well as much useful advice and information on entry to the UK, funding and scholarships, and other relevant topics.

For those specifically interested in teacher education, a good guide to teaching as a career, and the various routes to achieving qualified-teacher status, is provided on the Teacher Training Agency (TTA) website.[25]

References

1. *Whitaker's Almanack* (annual). London: The Stationery Office.
2. Lawton, D. and Gordon, P. (1996), *Dictionary of Education*, 2nd ed. London: Hodder & Stoughton.
3. Farrell, M., Kerry, T. and Kerry, C. (1995), *Blackwell Handbook of Education*. Oxford: Blackwell.
4. Gearon, L. (2002), *Education in the United Kingdom: Structures and organisation*. London: David Fulton.
5. Holt, G., Boyd, S., Dickinson, B., Loose, J. and O'Donnell, S. (1999), *Education in England, Wales and Northern Ireland: A guide to the system*, new ed. Slough: National Foundation for Educational Research.
6. Eurydice, *Eurybase 2001 The information database on education systems in Europe* http://www.eurydice.org
7. Husén, T. and Postlethwaite, T.N. eds (1994), *International Encyclopedia of Education: Research and studies*, 2nd ed. Oxford: Pergamon.
8. Postlethwaite, T.N. ed. (1995), *International Encyclopedia of National Systems of Education*, 2nd ed. Oxford: Elsevier.
9. Husén, T. (1998), *Education: The complete encyclopedia* (CD-ROM). Oxford: Pergamon.
10. Department for Education and Skills: Teachernet, *UK Education system* http://www.teachernet.gov.uk/educationoverview/uksystem
11. British Council, *Education UK* http://www.educationuk.org
12. British Council, *Education UK Scotland* http://www.educationukscotland.org
13. BBC *Guide to the UK's education systems* http://news.bbc.co.uk/1/hi/education/uk_systems
14. Chitty, C. (1999), *The Education System Transformed*, 2nd ed. Tisbury: Baseline Book Company.
15. MacKinnon, D. and Statham, J. (1999), *Education in the UK: Facts and figures*, 3rd ed. London: Hodder & Stoughton in association with the Open University.
16. Department for Education and Employment (1999), *The National Curriculum for England. Handbook for primary teachers in England: key stages 1 and 2*. London: The Stationery Office for DfEE and QCA.
17. Department for Education and Employment (1999), *The National*

Curriculum for England. Handbook for secondary teachers in England: key stages 3 and 4. London: The Stationery Office for DfEE and QCA.

18. Qualifications and Curriculum Authority, *National Curriculum online* http://www.nc.uk.net
19. Qualifications, Curriculum and Assessment Authority for Wales http://www.accac.org.uk
20. Learning and Teaching Scotland http://www.ltscotland.com
21. Gold, R. and Szemerenyi, S. (annual), *Running a School: Legal duties and responsibilities*. Bristol: Jordan Publishing.
22. Department for Education and Skills (2001), *National Literacy Strategy: Framework for teaching*, 3rd ed. London: DfES.
23. Department for Education and Employment. Standards and Effectiveness Unit (1999), *The National Numeracy Strategy. Framework for teaching mathematics, from reception to year 6*. London: DfEE.
24. Department for Education and Skills, *The standards site* http://www.standards.dfes.gov.uk
25. Teacher Training Agency http://www.canteach.gov.uk

3 The qualifications maze

Key questions:
How do I find out about different GCSE exam boards? What is the International Baccalaureate? What is the difference between a GNVQ and an A level? Will universities accept AS levels? What if I disagree with my exam results? What are key skills? Will my qualifications be good enough to get into a university abroad?

The qualifications system in the UK has changed considerably over the last 15 years, so that many British people, as well as potential students from overseas, may need help in discovering what qualifications are currently available, and how they relate to each other. A brief outline of the system appears in *Whitaker's Almanack*;[1] more detail is provided in specialist sources such as *Education in England, Wales and Northern Ireland: A guide to the system*,[2] which is also available online through *Eurybase*.[3] The British Council's *International Guide to Qualifications in Education*[4] also provides a good overview of the system, and briefer details can be found on their *Education UK* website.[5]

Alternatively, definitions of individual terms can be found in dictionaries and glossaries. Lawton and Gordon's *Dictionary of Education*[6] gives clear explanations of terms such as National Vocational Qualification or International Baccalaureate. A much wider range of qualifications, from all over Europe, is covered by the Eurydice *European Glossary on Education, Vol. 1: Examinations, qualifications and titles*.[7] As well as an alphabetical listing, with details of each examination, it gives a summary in table form for each country. It includes qualifications for school and higher education up to postgraduate level.

School examinations

For more detailed information on school examinations in the UK, the key starting point is the Qualification and Curriculum Authority's (QCA) website.[8] This includes detailed descriptions of the national qualifications framework and the requirements of the various elements within it, as well as related information on other aspects of the school curriculum. It also provides a news section giving the latest updates, press releases and reports. The Department for Education and Skills (DfES) website also has a section on qualifications covering the school and 16–19 examination systems.[9] It includes the latest news and government statements on qualifications.

A fuller introduction to the public examinations system, and especially the work of the examining boards, is provided by Lloyd's *How Exams Really Work*.[10] This is a good source of information on such topics as support for children with disabilities, conduct of appeals and problems of cheating in coursework and examinations. The individual examining boards – Assessment and Qualifications Alliance (AQA);[11] Edexcel;[12] Oxford, Cambridge and RSA Examinations (OCR);[13] Northern Ireland Council for the Curriculum, Examinations and Assessment (CCEA);[14] and Welsh Joint Education Committee[15] – all have their own websites, giving details of their work, publications and latest developments. In addition, there is a website for the Examination Appeals Board (EAB),[16] described as 'an independent body, set up by Ministers in 1999, to help give confidence to candidates, parents, schools and colleges who make use of the examinations system that the grades awarded are fair and accurate'. It deals with the final stages of the enquiries and appeals process.

For details of the examination system in Scotland, which differs in many respects from that in England and Wales, the British Council's *Education UK Scotland* website[17] gives an overview. The Scottish Qualifications Authority (SQA)[18] also hosts a website, covering qualifications other than degrees.

Post-school qualifications

Beyond school level, qualifications tend to divide between the academic and the vocational. One standard publication which covers both aspects, but with more emphasis on the academic and professional side, is the regularly updated *British Qualifications*.[19] This includes an outline of school examinations, and of qualifications obtained through further education and the university system, including a listing of the courses offered by individual universities. A further section then deals with membership of professional bodies, giving the qualifications offered at all levels for a range of professions and occupations.

On the academic side, the Higher Education Funding Council for England (HEFCE) produce an outline of undergraduate and postgraduate qualifications, *Higher education in the United Kingdom*.[20] Details of courses and entry requirements are provided by the Universities and Colleges Admissions Service for the UK (UCAS) in *The official guide*,[21] and on their website.[22] (More details of this and other sources of information on universities are given in Chapter 4.)

Vocational qualifications are covered in some detail by another publication, *British Vocational Qualifications*.[23] The main part of this work provides an extensive listing of the qualifications available for a wide range of careers and occupations. There are also useful sections on awarding bodies and on colleges offering vocational courses. For further details of National Vocational Qualifications (NVQs), the DfES website[9] offers full details of the qualifications offered and how to obtain them. Information on lifelong learning also often has a vocational emphasis. The DfES *Adult learners' gateway*[24] gives a wider overview, with useful links to both DfES pages and other sites concerned with adult learning at all levels, including the National Institute of Adult Continuing Education (NIACE),[25] Learndirect[26] and the Basic Skills Agency.[27]

International equivalence

Growing opportunities for both studying and working abroad make enquiries about the equivalence of qualifications from different countries increasingly common. The standard reference book is the British Council's *International*

Guide to Qualifications in Education.[4] Besides outlining the education and qualification systems of 165 countries, this makes explicit comparisons with British qualifications. Some information about equivalence of qualifications is also included on the British Council website.[5] For queries concerning Europe, the European Community (EC) publication *A Guide to Higher Education Systems and Qualifications in the EU and EEA Countries*[28] is also useful. It provides detailed accounts of higher education in member states, but does not indicate direct equivalence of qualifications. Information on European vocational qualifications is available from the European Centre for the Development of Vocational Training (CEDEFOP),[29] which hosts an extensive website designed to provide 'the latest information on the present state of and future trends in vocational education and training in the European Union' (EU).

Advice on equivalence of qualifications is available from the National Academic Recognition Information Centre (NARIC),[30] operated by ECCTIS Ltd under contract to the DfES. They offer an advisory service on academic qualifications available to individuals as well as institutions.

References

1. *Whitaker's Almanack* (annual). London: The Stationery Office.
2. Holt, G., Boyd, S., Dickinson, B., Loose, J. and O'Donnell, S. (1999), *Education in England, Wales and Northern Ireland: A guide to the system*, new ed. Slough: National Foundation for Educational Research.
3. Eurydice, *Eurybase 2001 The information database on education systems in Europe* http://www.eurydice.org
4. British Council (1996), *International Guide to Qualifications in Education*, 4th ed. London: British Council, National Academic Recognition Information Centre for the United Kingdom.
5. British Council, *UK Education and training systems* http://www.britishcouncil.org/education/system
6. Lawton, D. and Gordon, P. (1996), *Dictionary of Education*, 2nd ed. London: Hodder & Stoughton.
7. Eurydice European Unit (1999), *European Glossary on Education. Vol. 1: Examinations, qualifications and titles.* Brussels: Eurydice European Unit.
8. Qualifications and Curriculum Authority http://www.qca.org.uk

9. Department for Education and Skills, *Qualifications for schools and colleges* http://www.dfes.gov.uk/qualifications

10. Lloyd, J.G. (1999), *How Exams Really Work: The Cassell guide to GCSEs, AS and A Levels*. London: Cassell.

11. Assessment and Qualifications Alliance http://www.aqa.org.uk

12. Edexcel http://www.edexcel.org.uk

13. Oxford, Cambridge and RSA Examinations http://www.ocr.org.uk

14. Northern Ireland Council for the Curriculum, Examinations and Assessment http://www.ccea.org.uk

15. Welsh Joint Education Committee http://www.wjec.co.uk

16. Examinations Appeals Board http://www.theeab.org.uk

17. British Council, *Education UK Scotland* http://www.educationukscotland.org

18. Scottish Qualifications Authority http://www.sqa.org.uk

19. *British Qualifications: A complete guide to educational, technical, professional and academic qualifications in Britain* (annual). London: Kogan Page.

20. Higher Education Funding Council for England (1999), *Higher education in the United Kingdom* http://www.hefce.ac.uk/Pubs/HEFCE/ 1999/99_02.htm

21. Universities and Colleges Admissions Service for the UK (annual), *University and College Entrance: The official guide* (sometimes entitled *The big guide*). Cheltenham: UCAS.

22. Universities and Colleges Admissions Service for the UK, *UCAS directory online* http://www.ucas.ac.uk

23. *British Vocational Qualifications: A directory of vocational qualifications available in the UK* (annual). London: Kogan Page.

24. Department for Education and Skills, *Adult learners' gateway* http://www.dfes.gov.uk/adultlearners

25. National Institute of Adult Continuing Education http://www.niace.org.uk

26. University for Industry, *Learndirect* http://www.learndirect.co.uk

27. Basic Skills Agency http://www.basic-skills.co.uk

28. Commission of the European Communities. Directorate-General for Education Training and Youth (1998), *A Guide to Higher Education Systems and Qualifications in the EU and EEA Countries*, 2nd ed. Luxembourg: Office for Official Publications of the European Community.

29. European Centre for the Development of Vocational Training http://www.cedefop.gr
30. National Academic Recognition Information Centre for the United Kingdom, *UK NARIC* http://www.naric.org.uk

4 Choosing a school or university

Key questions:
What schools are there in this area? Where did they come in the league tables? How can I find out about private schools? Where can I study aeronautical engineering? Are there any part-time courses in creative writing? How do I know who teaches on the course?

Many people need information about individual schools, universities or other educational institutions. The simplest questions are those which ask for basic contact details for a named institution; more complex queries require comparative information on a range of establishments in a particular geographical area, or details of courses in a given subject area. Fortunately, a wide range of directories and websites exists to provide this information, and there are also an increasing number of tools offering comparative or evaluative data.

Schools

Two directories include basic address and contact information for all post-primary educational establishments in the UK. *Education Year Book*[1] covers central and local government education departments, with details of the schools they control, and also has sections on independent schools, on higher and vocational education, and details of educational organisations. *The Education Authorities Directory and Annual*[2] contains the same information, but presented in a slightly different order, bringing together all institutions of the same type, such as secondary schools, special schools, and professional development centres. Either is a useful source for the many straightforward enquiries which seek only name, address and telephone number; and their geographical arrangement, by local education authority (LEA), also allows for easy identification of schools in a particular area. Primary schools are not included in the above, but are comprehensively listed in *The Primary Education Directory*,[3] which gives a similar level of information for all primary schools, state and independent, throughout the UK. *The Special Education Directory*[4] is a similar production, from the same publisher, covering special schools.

The independent sector has long been covered by a range of directories which aim to help with the choice of school. *Which School?*,[5] for instance, provides a basic directory of address and fee information, supplemented by numerous advertisements. The same publisher produces a range of more specialist directories (*Which School? at Sixteen*,[6] and *Which School? for Special Needs*,[7] for instance) and also offers information by way of a website.[8] In similar vein, *The Independent Schools Guide*[9] is produced by long-established educational consultants Gabbitas, and *The Guide to Independent Schools*[10] (previously *The Equitable Schools Book*) published by Trotman, is also a long-running publication, reaching its 14th edition in 2002.

More recently, listings have appeared which cover both state and independent schools. *The Daily Telegraph Schools Guide*[11] describes itself as 'the definitive guide to the best independent and state schools', providing information about schools which have been visited and assessed independently, rather than publishing entries written by the schools. Two companion guides by Robert Findlay, *Choose the Right Primary School*[12] and *Choose the Right Secondary School*,[13] in addition to background information on the education system as a whole, provide extensive tables of comparative data – including the Standard Assessment Tasks (SATs) statistics for primary schools, and examination results and truancy rates for secondary schools.

School performance

For those wanting more detailed information, a number of important websites provide access to school performance tables and to inspection reports. School performance tables (league tables) for secondary schools, showing the results of public examinations, were first published in 1992. The tables for England are now available online on the Department for Education and Skills (DfES) web pages, *Statistics* section.[14] This website contains information on examination results and rates of absence for secondary schools from 1994, and for primary schools (based on the key stage 2 tests) from 1996. Inspection reports, giving more detailed assessments of all aspects of a school, are also available through the web. The Office for Standards in Education (Ofsted) website[15] includes full text (in Adobe pdf format) of nursery, school and college reports for England. In Wales the National Assembly for Wales provides secondary school performance tables on the *Learning Wales*[16] section of its website. Welsh school inspection reports are available from the Estyn[17] website.

Further and higher education

Enquiries in the further and higher education sectors tend to focus more frequently on information about courses in particular subject areas, rather than general information about an institution as a whole. Basic information is included in the *Education Year Book*[1] and *The Education Authorities Directory and Annual*,[2] above, and specialist directories such as the *Directory of Vocational and Further Education*,[18] which includes details of central and local government education departments, and of colleges and examination boards. In the university sector, address and contact details are included in a number of international directories such as the *Commonwealth Universities Yearbook*,[19] *The World of Learning*[20] and the *International Handbook of Universities*.[21] Publications such as *The Push Guide to Which University*[22] aim to provide more detailed information about each institution, from the point of view of prospective students.

Arrangement by subject and course is available for further education in the *Directory of Vocational and Further Education*,[18] and for UK universities through *The official guide*,[23] which includes information on how to apply for undergraduate courses. This information is also made available through the *UCAS directory online*.[24] Postgraduate courses are covered by *Prospects Postgraduate Directory*,[25] the official guide produced by Universities UK. For those concerned about entry requirements, *Degree*

Course Offers[26] provides an annual survey of the examination grades required to obtain a place on a degree course. The British Council publish a guide called *Access to UK Higher Education,*[27] aimed at overseas applicants. Fuller information for overseas students is available from their *Education UK*[28] website.

Quality assessment

Further information on the quality of provision in further and higher education is again available on the web. In higher education, the Quality Assurance Agency (QAA) website[29] provides Subject Review/Quality Assessment reports, looking at individual subjects within an institution, as well as reports on institutional reviews, for higher education institutions in England and Northern Ireland. Academic Review reports for institutions in Scotland from 2000 to 2001 can also be found on the QAA site. Quality Assessment reports for institutions in Scotland from 1992 to 1998 can be found on the Scottish Higher Education Funding Council site.[30] Assessment profiles for institutions in Wales can be found on the Higher Education Funding Council for Wales site.[31]

Teacher training, however, comes under the aegis of the Teacher Training Agency (TTA),[32] and is inspected by Ofsted. Reports for institutions in England are on the Ofsted site.[33]

References

1. *Education Year Book* (annual). London: Longman for the Association of Education Committees.
2. *The Education Authorities Directory and Annual* (annual). Redhill: School Government Publishing.
3. *The Primary Education Directory* (annual). Redhill: School Government Publishing Company.
4. *The Special Education Directory* (annual). Redhill: School Government Publishing Company.
5. Gabbitas Truman & Thring Educational Trust (annual), *Which School?* Saxmundham: John Catt.

6. Gabbitas Truman & Thring Educational Trust (annual), *Which School? at Sixteen.* Saxmundham: John Catt.
7. Gabbitas Truman & Thring Educational Trust (annual), *Which School? for Special Needs: A guide to independent and non-maintained schools.* Saxmundham: John Catt.
8. John Catt Educational, *John Catt's Schoolsearch* http://www.schoolsearch.co.uk
9. Gabbitas Educational Consultants (annual), *The Independent Schools Guide.* London: Kogan Page.
10. Boehm, K. ed. (annual), *The Guide to Independent Schools.* Richmond: Trotman.
11. Clare, J. ed. (1998), *The Daily Telegraph Schools Guide 1998–99: The definitive guide to the best independent and state schools.* London: Robinson.
12. Findlay, R. (1998), *Choose the Right Primary School: A guide to primary schools in England, Scotland and Wales.* London: The Stationery Office.
13. Findlay, R. (1998), *Choose the Right Secondary School: A guide to secondary schools in England, Scotland and Wales.* London: The Stationery Office.
14. Department for Education and Skills, *DfES school and college performance tables* http://www.dfes.gov.uk/performancetables
15. Office for Standards in Education, *Reports* http://www.ofsted.gov.uk/reports
16. National Assembly for Wales, *Learning Wales* http://www.learning.wales.gov.uk
17. Estyn: Her Majesty's Inspectorate for Education and Training in Wales http://www.estyn.gov.uk
18. *Directory of Vocational and Further Education* (annual). London: Pitman.
19. Association of Commonwealth Universities (annual), *Commonwealth Universities Yearbook: A directory to the universities of the Commonwealth and the handbook of their Association.* London: Association of Commonwealth Universities.
20. *The World of Learning* (annual). London: Europa.
21. International Association of Universities (biennial), *International Handbook of Universities: And other institutions of higher education.* London: Macmillan.

22. McCaffrey, K. (annual), *The Push Guide to Which University*. London: The Stationery Office.
23. Universities and Colleges Admissions Service for the UK (annual), *University and College Entrance: The official guide* (sometimes entitled *The big guide*). Cheltenham: UCAS.
24. Universities and Colleges Admissions Service for the UK, *UCAS directory online* http://www.ucas.ac.uk
25. Higher Education Careers Services Unit (2000), *Prospects Postgraduate Directory: The official guide, with over 4,500 UK courses and research opportunities*. Manchester: CSU.
26. *The Complete Degree Course Offers: The comprehensive guide on entry to universities and colleges* (annual). Richmond: Trotman.
27. British Council (1996/8), *Access to UK Higher Education: A guide for international students*. London: HMSO.
28. British Council, *Education UK* http://www.educationuk.org
29. Quality Assurance Agency for Higher Education, *Review reports* http://www.qaa.ac.uk/revreps/reviewreports.htm
30. Scottish Higher Education Funding Council http://www.shefc.ac.uk
31. Higher Education Funding Council for Wales http://www.wfc.ac.uk/hefcw
32. Teacher Training Agency http://www.canteach.gov.uk
33. Office for Standards in Education http://www.ofsted.gov.uk

5 The legal framework

Key questions:
What major reports have there been in the last three years? What is government policy on selection? Can I educate my child at home? Has the school the right to send my child home? What are the head-teacher's legal responsibilities?

Education is one of the most highly regulated areas of modern life. Over recent years, a succession of reports and Education Acts – with their accompanying regulations (usually in the form of Statutory Instruments) – Circulars and other guidance, have made finding information on legislation or official policy an increasingly difficult proposition. The complexity of the material and the frequency of change, not only in the legislative framework but also in the way in which government information is presented to the public, make it difficult to be certain of finding full and accurate information. The advent of the internet, with its potential for providing really up-to-date information, provides some assistance in this field, though even here it is not always as easy as one might wish to locate exactly what is needed.

Lists and summaries

The first problem is often one of identifying the exact document wanted from incomplete information. Many Education Acts are distinguished only by their date, an easy source of confusion; major education reports, often the seminal documents on which legislation is later based, are commonly referred to by the names of their chairpersons, not by their official titles. Clear lists and summaries of official documents are surprisingly difficult to find. *Education in the UK: Facts and figures*[1] includes two useful chapters: one covers major official reports from 1944 to 1997, with both popular and official titles, and brief summaries of their contents; the other covers legislation from 1870 to 1998. Both chapters are selective. *Education Year Book 2002/03*[2] contains a list of legislation from 1962 to 2001, with brief summaries of the contents of each Act. Earlier editions of *Education Year Book* also contained a brief list of government reports (from 1944 to 1989 in the 1999/2000 edition) but this has been dropped from the later versions. For earlier materials (to 1984), Maclure's *Educational Documents: England and Wales, 1816 to the present day*[3] provides a rather fuller overview, giving extracts from the documents themselves rather than merely summarising them. Once again, only a selection of the most important is included.

Finding the full text

Once the document has been identified, a copy of the full text may be required. Longer documents, such as committee of enquiry reports, must be treated as individual items and located through library catalogues. The standard printed source for legislation is *The Law of Education*,[4] a regularly updated looseleaf publication, now running to six volumes, which includes the text of all legislation currently in force. Individual items are of course published separately by Her Majesty's Stationery Office (HMSO).

Online, the website of HMSO[5] provides access to the text of all Acts of Parliament since 1988, and of Statutory Instruments since 1987. The HMSO website also includes information about Command papers, and links to internet versions where published. (Consultative documents such as white papers and green papers are usually published as Command papers.) The main source for Command papers is the website of The Stationery Office (TSO): *Official Documents*,[6] which includes a comprehensive list for the current year and an archive from 1994. For legislation currently before Parliament, the UK Parliament website[7] provides access to papers from both the House of Lords and the House of Commons, including draft legislation (Bills) and Hansard.

Topical information

A frequent problem in this area is identifying and locating copies of very topical material, which often receives coverage in the press. Here, the online sources are most likely to provide the information required. In addition to the general government sites, the Department for Education and Skills (DfES) website[8] is the most obvious starting point. It includes news, publications, speeches, consultations and statistics. The publications listed are those produced by the DfES itself, some published through TSO and others distributed direct. The *Guidance on the law archive*[9] covers what were known as Department for Education and Employment (DfEE) Circulars until 2001. From that date guidance is included on the *Teachernet* section of the website,[10] under the heading *Guidance and legislation*.

Other useful websites include those of government agencies such as the Qualifications and Curriculum Authority (QCA), and the Office for Standards in Education (Ofsted). The QCA website[11] includes information on curriculum, assessment and public qualifications (see Chapter 3). The QCA is also responsible for the *National Curriculum* website,[12] which includes the text of the National Curriculum as well as schemes of work, support materials from the QCA and the government, and links to teaching resources. The Ofsted website[13] provides access to its many publications, including both reports on individual schools and guidance and discussion documents on a wide range of topics, as well as its latest press releases. Other sites which cover important areas of official policy for education include the DfES *Standards site*,[14] which covers standards and assessment, and the Teacher Training Agency (TTA) site,[15] for all matters concerned with teacher education. The DfES *Links* page[16] provides an extensive list of links to other sites in the field of education.

Guidance and interpretation

For many queries, access to the text of official documents will not be sufficient on its own: some kind of guidance or interpretation will be more appropriate. In addition to the assistance offered on the official sites listed above, a number of other organisations offer guidance. The most important of these is the Advisory Centre for Education (ACE),[17] which provides news, information and advice for parents, school governors and teachers through its website and publications. Its website includes a brief but useful list of frequently asked questions (mainly aimed at parents). Publications include a series of guides for parents, governors and schools, and summaries of recent major Education Acts. It is a good source of information on special educational needs (SEN), and the implication of the much quoted *Code of Practice*.[18] In a more specialised area, the Home Education Advisory Service (HEAS) provides useful advice for parents contemplating educating their children outside the school system. Again, it has a website,[19] and produces publications including the *Home Education Handbook*[20] and leaflets on specific topics.

Both these organisations place a lot of emphasis on guidance for parents. Other publications, especially books, tend to be aimed at a particular, often professional, audience. Thus *The Head's Legal Guide*[21] is a guide to the legal responsibilities of headteachers. It appears in print as a looseleaf volume, supplemented by fortnightly *Headteacher's briefings* and *Teacher's briefings*, and a bi-monthly *Headteacher's bulletin*. It is also available on CD-ROM. From the same publisher come two other looseleaf guides on the same lines: the *Manual for Heads of Science*[22] and the *School Governor's Manual*.[23] In somewhat the same vein is the useful *Running a School 2002/03: Legal duties and responsibilities*,[24] this time a book revised annually. *Teachers' Legal Liabilities and Responsibilities: The Bristol guide*[25] is a useful brief guide to this area.

Expert advice

All the sites and publications listed above are mainly concerned to provide information on the law and government policy for the layman, whether parent or teacher. Where there is any question of a legal dispute, expert advice is essential, and questions should be referred to other appropriate agencies. For parents, ACE would be a good starting point. For teachers, the services of one of the teachers' unions or professional associations would be the obvious first choice.

The law in practice

Finally, there is no shortage of information for the legal practitioner or law student. Recent books include Hyams' *Law of Education*[26] and Ford, Hughes and Ruebain's *Education Law and Practice*.[27] A number of journals are devoted specifically to education law. *Education and the Law*[28] includes articles and a current survey of statutes, Statutory Instruments, case law, and ombudsman reports; *Education Law Journal*[29] follows a similar format. *Education, Public Law and the Individual*[30] concentrates on articles, with brief case synopses. Full reports of education law cases are provided by *Education Law Reports*.[31]

References

1. MacKinnon, D. and Statham, J. (1999), *Education in the UK: Facts and figures*, 3rd ed. London: Hodder & Stoughton in association with the Open University.
2. *Education Year Book* (annual). London: Longman for the Association of Education Committees.
3. Maclure, S. (1985), *Educational Documents: England and Wales, 1816 to the present day*, 5th ed. London: Methuen.
4. Liell, P., Saunders, J.B. and Taylor, G. eds (1984–), *The Law of Education*, 9th ed. London: Butterworths.
5. Her Majesty's Stationery Office http://www.hmso.gov.uk
6. The Stationery Office, *Official documents* http://www.official-documents.co.uk
7. The United Kingdom Parliament http://www.parliament.uk
8. Department for Education and Skills http://www.dfes.gov.uk
9. Department for Education and Skills, *Guidance on the law* http://www.dfes.gov.uk/publications/guidanceonthelaw
10. Department for Education and Skills, *Teachernet* http://www.teachernet.gov.uk
11. Qualifications and Curriculum Authority http://www.qca.org.uk
12. Qualifications and Curriculum Authority, *National Curriculum online* http://www.nc.uk.net
13. Office for Standards in Education http://www.ofsted.gov.uk

14. Department for Education and Skills, *The Standards site* http://www.standards.dfes.gov.uk
15. Teacher Training Agency http://www.canteach.gov.uk
16. Department for Education and Skills, *Links* http://www.dfes.gov.uk/ links.shtml
17. Advisory Centre for Education http://www.ace-ed.org.uk
18. Department for Education and Skills (2001), *Special Educational Needs Code of Practice*. Annesley: DfES Publications.
19. Home Education Advisory Service http://www.heas.org.uk
20. Lowe, J. (1998), *The Home Education Handbook: A practical guide to home education*. Welwyn Garden City: Home Education Advisory Service.
21. Howarth, S.B. (1984–), *The Head's Legal Guide*. New Malden: Croner.
22. *Croner's Manual for Heads of Science* (1991–), Kingston upon Thames: Croner.
23. *School Governor's Manual* (1992–), Kingston upon Thames: Croner.
24. Gold, R. and Szemerenyi, S. (annual), *Running a School: Legal duties and responsibilities*. Bristol: Jordan Publishing.
25. University of Bristol Graduate School of Education (2002), *Teachers' Legal Liabilities and Responsibilities: The Bristol guide*, revised and extended ed. Bristol: University of Bristol Graduate School of Education.
26. Hyams, O. (1998), *Law of Education*. London: Sweet & Maxwell.
27. Ford, J., Hughes, M. and Ruebain, D. (1999), *Education Law and Practice*. London: Legal Action Group.
28. *Education and the Law* (1989–). Harlow: Longman.
29. *Education Law Journal* (2000–). Bristol: Jordan Publishing.
30. *Education, Public Law and the Individual* (1996–). Bognor Regis: John Wiley & Sons.
31. *Education Law Reports* (1994–). Bristol: Jordan Publishing.

6 Equal opportunities and inclusive education

Key questions:
What does it mean if my child is statemented? What is inclusive education? How can I find out about special schools? What is the Code of Practice? What does the Race Relations Amendment Act say about education?

Questions about equal opportunities and inclusion continue to raise topical and at times emotive issues. What exactly do we mean by inclusive education, and how does it work in practice? An increasing amount of information on these issues, especially with regard to special needs and disability, is now available, much of it through the internet.

Race and gender

Issues around race and gender discrimination have generated many reports and recommendations over a long period: among the most recent, the report of the Stephen Lawrence inquiry[1] includes sections on education and is also available online.[2] The Commission for Racial Equality (CRE) website[3] provides a wide range of information around issues of race and ethnicity, including legal information. The Home Office website has a section on *Race equality and diversity*[4] which offers links to other sites and to relevant publications. These include the *Race Relations (Amendment) Act*,[5] which has provisions concerning education. The Department for Education and Skills (DfES) *Standards* site has a section on *Ethnic minority achievement*[6] that is intended to support schools and local education authorities (LEAs) by sharing examples of good practice and by providing useful links to further information and research on minority ethnic pupils' educational achievement.

A useful source for definitions and basic concepts is the *Dictionary of Multicultural Education*,[7] edited by Grant and Ladson-Billings. This includes definitions and brief discussions of terms such as 'feminism', 'multiculturalism', 'political correctness', 'integration' and many others.

On gender issues, the *Gender and achievement* pages on the DfES *Standards* site[8] include case studies and also provide up-to-date information and an overview of recent research. Official statistics (see Chapter 7) also provide useful source material for discussion, especially for issues of gender and achievement.

Special education and disability

The term 'inclusion' or 'inclusive education' is also used widely in the context of special education and disability. An excellent first source for information on the whole area is the website provided by the Centre for Studies on Inclusive Education (CSIE)[9] at the University of the West of England. This covers *Inclusion basics*, such as definitions, the more detailed *Inclusion information guide*, sections on inclusion in the UK and international links. It also provides information about the CSIE publication *Index for Inclusion: Developing learning and participation in schools*.[10] This is not an index of the dictionary type, but 'a set of materials to guide schools through a process of inclusive school development'. The DfES has funded the distribution of the *Index* to every school and LEA in England.

For greater depth in the special needs area, a recent and comprehensive textbook is Frederickson and Cline's *Special Educational Needs, Inclusion and Diversity*.[11]

Special needs is the sole focus of the useful website provided by the National Association for Special Educational Needs (NASEN).[12] Besides information about the organisation and its activities, the website includes Position Statements, policies and press releases. Members of NASEN may also access the research database of current and recently completed research on special needs in the UK. NASEN publish two well-established journals of great importance for teachers and researchers: *Support for Learning*[13] and the *British Journal of Special Education.*[14] They have recently introduced a refereed online journal, the *Journal of research in special educational needs.*[15]

Official policy and legal requirements for inclusion are covered by a range of publications and websites. General manuals covering the legal responsibilities of headteachers and governors include these issues. *Running a School 2002/03: Legal duties and responsibilities,*[16] for instance, has two chapters, on special educational needs (SEN) and disability discrimination, as well as references to discrimination in sections on admissions and discipline. (See Chapter 5 for other sources for the law of education.) The *SEN Code of Practice,*[17] from the DfES, provides practical advice to LEAs, schools and others on carrying out their statutory duties in providing for SEN in England. It was revised and updated in 2001, and is available on the DfES website,[18] as well as in printed form. A range of other documents is also available from this site. *Inclusive schooling – children with special educational needs,*[19] for instance, provides practical guidance on the new statutory framework for inclusion. The equivalent document for Wales is the *SEN Code of Practice for Wales* (2002), available on the National Assembly for Wales *Learning Wales* website.[20] Information on SEN in Scotland is available on the Scottish Executive website.[21]

In a wider context, the *Disability Discrimination Act*[22] can be found online on the government's *Disability* website. Other education sites also include pages on inclusion. The National Grid for Learning pages provide *Inclusion, a catalogue of on-line resources to support individual learning needs;*[23] the *National Curriculum online* site[24] includes a general statement on inclusion and a range of support materials and links to further resources.

Schools and colleges

Equal opportunity issues may also be a factor in questions about choosing a school or college. The general guides and directories listed in Chapter 4 should include information on such areas as single-sex or co-education, and religious affiliation. Searching for such items, as well as other special factors, may be easier on the related websites: the Independent Schools of the British Isles (ISBI) site, *ISBI the database,*[25] for instance, allows for searching by different categories of special needs as well as special facilities and religious affiliation.

Special needs are also covered by a range of specialist directories. *The Special Education Directory*[26] is a comprehensive listing of both maintained and independent schools which make provision for special needs, arranged by geographical area and providing basic contact details; the *Gabbitas Guide to Schools for Special Needs*[27] also covers both state and independent schools, and provides a substantial section of guidance for parents, explaining the system. *Which School? for Special Needs*[28] is a guide to independent schools. At the college level, the Association of National Specialist Colleges (NATSPEC) *Directory*[29] is produced by an organisation whose members offer education and training for young people and adults with learning difficulties and/or disabilities.

Other organisations

Useful information on special needs and disability issues is also offered by a range of other organisations, most easily explored through their websites. The Alliance for Inclusive Education (Allfie)[30] is a membership organisation for individuals, families and groups committed to inclusive ideals; the Basic Skills Agency[31] is the national agency promoting literacy and basic skills for adults. TechDis[32] is a Joint Information Systems Committee (JISC) funded service supporting the further and higher education community in all aspects of technology and disability; Skill: National Bureau for Students with Disabilities[33] promotes opportunities for young people and adults with any kind of disability in post-16 education, training and employment across the UK. The British Educational Communications and Technology (Becta) *Inclusion* site[34] looks at the use of Information and Communications Technology (ICT) to promote inclusion. For those concerned with teacher training, useful links and information are available from the Special Educational Needs Joint Initiative for Training (SENJIT) at the Institute of Education,[35] and the Teacher Training Agency (TTA)[36] also includes some information on its pages.

References

1. Macpherson of Cluny, Sir William (chairman) (1999), *The Stephen Lawrence Inquiry (report of an inquiry)*. London: The Stationery Office.
2. Macpherson of Cluny, Sir William (chairman), *The Stephen Lawrence Inquiry (report of an inquiry)* http://www.archive.official-documents.co.uk/document/cm42/4262/4262.htm
3. Commission for Racial Equality http://www.cre.gov.uk
4. Home Office, *Race equality and diversity* http://www.homeoffice.gov.uk/new_indexs/index_racial-equality.htm
5. Home Office *Race Relations (Amendment) Act 2000 and the EC Article 13 Race Directive* http://www.homeoffice.gov.uk/raceact/welcome.htm
6. Department for Education and Skills, *Ethnic minority achievement* http://www.standards.dfee.gov.uk/ethnicminorities
7. Grant, C.A. and Ladson-Billings, G. eds (1997), *Dictionary of Multicultural Education*. Phoenix, Ariz.: Oryx Press.
8. Department for Education and Skills, *Gender and achievement* http://www.standards.dfee.gov.uk/genderandachievement
9. Centre for Studies on Inclusive Education http://inclusion.uwe.ac.uk
10. Booth, T. and Ainscow, M. (2002), *Index for Inclusion: Developing learning and participation in schools*, revised ed. Bristol: Centre for Studies on Inclusive Education, University of the West of England.
11. Frederickson, N. and Cline, T. (2002), *Special Educational Needs, Inclusion and Diversity: A textbook*. Buckingham: Open University Press.
12. National Association for Special Educational Needs http://www.nasen.org.uk
13. National Association for Special Educational Needs (1986–), *Support for Learning*. Oxford: Blackwell.
14. National Association for Special Educational Needs (1985–), *British Journal of Special Education*. Tamworth: NASEN.
15. National Association for Special Educational Needs (2001–), *Journal of research in special educational needs* http://www.nasen.uk.com/ejournal
16. Gold, R. and Szemerenyi, S. (annual), *Running a School: Legal duties and responsibilities*. Bristol: Jordan Publishing.
17. Department for Education and Skills (2001), *Special Educational Needs Code of Practice*. Annesley: DfES Publications.

18. Department for Education and Skills, *Special educational needs code of practice* http://www.dfes.gov.uk/sen/viewDocument.cfm?dID=260

19. Department for Education and Skills, *Inclusive schooling – children with special educational needs* http://www.dfes.gov.uk/sen/viewDocument.cfm?dID=237

20. National Assembly for Wales, *Learning Wales* http://www.learning.wales.gov.uk

21. Scottish Executive, *Executive online* http://www.scotland.gov.uk

22. Department for Work and Pensions, *Disability Discrimination Act* http://www.disability.gov.uk/dda/act.html

23. National Grid for Learning, *Inclusion, a catalogue of on-line resources to support individual learning needs* http://inclusion.ngfl.gov.uk

24. Qualifications and Curriculum Authority, *National Curriculum online: Inclusion* http://www.nc.uk.net/inclus.html

25. Independent Schools of the British Isles, *ISBI the database* http://www.earl.org.uk/isbi

26. *The Special Education Directory* (annual). Redhill: School Government Publishing Company.

27. Gabbitas Educational Consultants (2000), *The Gabbitas Guide to Schools for Special Needs*, 6th ed. London: Kogan Page.

28. Gabbitas Truman & Thring Educational Trust (annual), *Which School? for Special Needs: A guide to independent and non-maintained schools*. Saxmundham: John Catt.

29. Association of National Specialist Colleges (2001), *Directory 2001 and 2002*. Association of National Specialist Colleges.

30. Alliance for Inclusive Education http://www.allfie.org.uk

31. Basic Skills Agency http://www.basic-skills.co.uk

32. TechDis http://www.techdis.ac.uk

33. Skill: National Bureau for Students with Disabilities http://www.skill.org.uk

34. British Educational Communications and Technology Agency, *Inclusion and special educational needs* http://www.becta.org.uk/inclusion

35. Special Educational Needs Joint Initiative for Training http://www.ioe.ac.uk/senjit

36. Teacher Training Agency http://www.canteach.gov.uk

7 Statistics

Key questions:
Where can I find examination results for the whole country for the last five years? How can I find out about education expenditure in different areas? How many teachers are there in UK primary schools? What are world literacy rates?

Finding statistics often appears a daunting task to the non-statistician. Questions range from one specific figure to wide-ranging comparisons across geographical areas and over periods of time. As always, finding current information can be problematical, particularly from conventional printed sources. Fortunately, the availability of internet sources has improved both the currency of information and the ease of searching for particular topics.

An understanding of the main sources available and who provides them is essential in finding relevant statistics. The best overview of the whole area is still the *Guide to Official Statistics*, from the Office for National Statistics,[1] which provides a comprehensive listing of statistics published by the government, and of the sources from which they are derived. *Online*, the National Statistics site,[2] aims to provide free access to a wide range of high-quality statistics. It is arranged by themes, one of which is education and training, and draws together information from a number of agencies.

Government statistics

The main provider of statistics for education is the Department for Education and Skills (DfES). Their key publication is *Education and Training Statistics for the United Kingdom,*[3] published annually since 1967. Each chapter has key facts, followed by a series of tables. Chapters cover expenditure, schools, post-compulsory education and training, qualifications, destinations, population, and international comparisons. The online version of this publication is available as a pdf file on the DfES *Statistics* web page,[4] listed under volumes.

For those wanting more detail, the DfES also produce a series of separate volumes under the general title of *Statistics of Education.* These currently include *Schools in England,*[5] *School workforce in England,*[6] *Public examinations GCSE/GNVQ and GCE/AGNVQ in England,*[7] and *Student support England and Wales.*[8] The *Statistics of Education* series has been published since 1966. Again, electronic versions of these volumes are available on the DfES *Statistics* website,[4] listed as volumes.

The DfES website also provides access to a range of other publications including *Statistical bulletins,*[9] *Statistical first releases*[10] and *Performance tables.*[11] It provides a list of key words for searching, such as exclusions or class sizes, as well as access to specific publications or broader categories. Particularly helpful for specific enquiries is the facility to search for local information by local education authority (LEA), ward or even postcode. The site includes a useful list of links to other sites offering statistical information, both UK and international.

Wales and Scotland

In addition to the volumes for England, statistics for Wales and Scotland are now published separately. For Wales, there are two annual volumes: *Schools in Wales: General statistics*[12] and *Schools in Wales: Examination performance.*[13] There is also a full selection of statistics on the website of the National Assembly for Wales.[14] For Scotland, see the statistics pages of the Scottish Executive website.[15]

Further and higher education

Higher education statistics are provided by the Higher Education Statistics Agency (HESA) in a series of annual publications. These include a summary volume, *Higher Education Statistics for the United Kingdom*,[16] and three more detailed analyses: *Resources of Higher Education Institutions*,[17] *Students in Higher Education Institutions*[18] and *First Destinations of Students Leaving Higher Education Institutions*.[19] *Higher Education Management Statistics. Sector level*[20] presents statistics showing a progression through higher education from the student's perspective, from applications through to first destinations. The HESA website[21] offers a full list of publications, and a more limited amount of free information.

Information for the further education sector has had a more chequered history since it ceased to be part of the *Statistics of Education* series. Formerly published by the Further Education Funding Council (FEFC), it is now provided by the Learning and Skills Council (LSC), and is available through their website.[22] *Summary Statistics for Further Education Institutions*[23] replaces *Performance Indicators* published by the FEFC. *Staff Statistics*[24] and *Student Statistics*[25] are also available.

Other organisations

In addition to the main government sources listed here, other groups provide further information on specific aspects of education. Full statistics of public examinations are published by the Joint Council for General Qualifications (JCGQ) on their website.[26] On the financial side, the Statistical Information Service of the Chartered Institute of Public Finance and Accountancy (CIPFA) produce two annual series, *Education Statistics: Estimates*[27] and *Education Statistics: Actuals*,[28] giving details of the education expenditure of LEAs.

National and international comparisons

Queries about education may sometimes need to be set in a wider context of national statistics. Apart from the wealth of information available through the National Statistics website,[2] a range of general statistical information is presented clearly and accessibly through their two long-running publications, *Social Trends*[29] and *Regional Trends*.[30] Both include charts and maps as well as tables, and cover social factors such as population, income and expenditure, housing, crime, health and environment.

As well as the national context, education statistics may also be seen in an international perspective. A worldwide summary of statistics was formerly provided by the *Unesco Statistical Yearbook*,[31] last edition 1999. Data are now available through their website.[32] European information can be found on the *Eurostat* website.[33] Their publications include *Key Data on Education in Europe*.[34] The statistics section of the Organisation for Economic Co-operation and Development (OECD) website[35] provides access to their education database, compiled from information supplied by member countries. The equivalent publication is *Education at a Glance*.[36]

A word of warning

All statistical publications need to be viewed with a certain caution. Sources such as those listed above, published by government or major international organisations, appear to be authoritative. In fact, the accuracy of the information they contain depends in part on the methods used to collect it, and it is always important to allow for the possibility of bias or incompleteness. Comparisons of figures from statistical tables are only valid if they have been compiled in the same way. The units used in tables can be confusing too: there is a big difference between 100s, 1,000s or even 1,000,000s. Finally, data are not always provided in exactly the format required: they may need to be worked on to reach the answer.

References

1. Office for National Statistics (irregular), *Guide to Official Statistics*. London: The Stationery Office.
2. National Statistics, *Online* http://www.statistics.gov.uk
3. Department for Education and Skills (annual), *Education and Training Statistics for the United Kingdom*. London: The Stationery Office.

4. Department for Education and Skills, *Statistical volumes* http://www.dfes.gov.uk/statistics/DB/VOL
5. Department for Education and Skills (irregular), *Statistics of Education: Schools in England*. London: The Stationery Office.
6. Department for Education and Skills (irregular), *Statistics of Education: School workforce in England*. London: The Stationery Office.
7. Department for Education and Skills (irregular), *Public Examinations GCSE/GNVQ and GCE/AGNVQ in England*. London: The Stationery Office.
8. Department for Education and Skills (irregular), *Student Support England and Wales*. London: The Stationery Office.
9. Department for Education and Skills, *Statistical bulletins* http://www.dfes.gov.uk/statistics/DB/SBU
10. Department for Education and Skills, *Statistical first releases* http://www.dfes.gov.uk/statistics/DB/SFR
11. Department for Education and Skills, *Statistics: performance tables* http://www.dfes.gov.uk/statistics/DB/PER
12. National Assembly for Wales (annual), *Schools in Wales: General statistics*. Cardiff: National Assembly for Wales.
13. National Assembly for Wales (annual), *Schools in Wales: Examination performance*. Cardiff: National Assembly for Wales.
14. National Assembly for Wales, *Statistics for Wales* http://www.wales.gov.uk/keypubstatisticsforwales
15. Scottish Executive, *Statistics in the Scottish Executive* http://www.scotland.gov.uk/stats
16. Higher Education Statistics Agency (annual), *Higher Education Statistics for the United Kingdom*. Cheltenham: HESA.
17. Higher Education Statistics Agency (annual), *Resources of Higher Education Institutions*. Cheltenham: HESA.
18. Higher Education Statistics Agency (annual), *Students in Higher Education Institutions*. Cheltenham: HESA.
19. Higher Education Statistics Agency (annual), *First Destinations of Students Leaving Higher Education Institutions*. Cheltenham: HESA.
20. Higher Education Statistics Agency (annual), *Higher Education Management Statistics. Sector level*. Cheltenham: HESA.
21. Higher Education Statistics Agency http://www.hesa.ac.uk
22. Learning and Skills Council http://www.lsc.gov.uk

23. Learning and Skills Council (annual), *Summary Statistics for Further Education Institutions*. London: LSC.
24. Learning and Skills Council (annual), *Staff Statistics*. London: LSC.
25. Learning and Skills Council (annual), *Student Statistics*. London: LSC.
26. Joint Council for General Qualifications http://www.jcgq.org.uk
27. Chartered Institute of Public Finance and Accountancy. Statistical Information Service (annual), *Education Statistics: Estimates*. London: CIPFA.
28. Chartered Institute of Public Finance and Accountancy. Statistical Information Service (annual), *Education Statistics: Actuals*. London: CIPFA.
29. Office for National Statistics (annual), *Social Trends*. London: National Statistics.
30. Office for National Statistics (annual), *Regional Trends*. London: National Statistics.
31. United Nations Educational Scientific and Cultural Organisation, *Unesco Statistical Yearbook*. Paris: Unesco Publishing and Bernan Press. Last published 1999.
32. United Nations Educational Scientific and Cultural Organisation http://www.unesco.org
33. Statistical Office of the European Communities, *Eurostat* http://europa.eu.int/comm/eurostat
34. Commission of the European Communities, Eurydice, and Commission of the European Communities Statistical Office (2000), *Key Data on Education in Europe*. Luxembourg: European Commission.
35. Organisation for Economic Co-operation and Development http://www.oecd.org
36. Organisation for Economic Co-operation and Development (annual), *Education at a Glance: OECD indicators*. London: The Stationery Office.

8 What's new?

Key questions:
What's the latest research on boys underachieving? How can I check on a television news story? What is the latest government initiative on teacher recruitment? Have this year's league tables been published yet?

News stories pose particular problems for the enquirer. A snippet of news, remembered out of context, offers very few clues on where to start looking for the full story. Current stories will be too new to appear in any index; older stories may still be missed because newspapers are not included, or not covered in detail, in more academic indexes. This is an area where access to electronic sources is vital, for both their greater currency and the much wider options for searching which they provide.

Current news

For stories currently in the news, the obvious starting point is still the weekly *Times Educational Supplement (TES)*,[1] offering comprehensive coverage of education matters, and its companion paper the *Times Higher Education Supplement (THES)*.[2] For a contrasting viewpoint, it may be worth looking at coverage of the same topic in other broadsheets, especially the *Education Guardian*[3] (published on Tuesdays) or *The Independent*.[4] All these papers also have websites (freely available except for the *THES*, which requires a subscription) which allow for searching by keyword, on the current site or the archive. The BUBL UK *Newspapers* page[5] provides a useful list of links to all UK papers, and some other news sources.

Current news is also very much the concern of the BBC, and the *Education* section of their BBC News website[6] is another excellent source for the latest headlines. The site is searchable, and covers news stories back to 1998.

Old news

Where the request is for press coverage of some past event or controversy, the electronic versions of papers are easily the most accessible sources. The archive on the *TES* website[7] is the best starting point, going back to 1994. The *Guardian*[8] archive is only from 1999 onwards, although the CD-ROM version of the paper has been available since 1991. Main feature articles in *TES* are indexed in *British Education Index*,[9] so this offers another option for tracing stories prior to 1994.

Press releases

News stories in education are often sparked off by some official announcement, new government report or initiative. A good source of information in this case is the official press release put out by the Department for Education and Skills (DfES), Office for Standards in Education (Ofsted), Qualifications and Curriculum Authority (QCA) or other official body. These can usually be found on the appropriate website. The DfES, for instance, now offers *News centre*,[10] which allows you to search the Press Notice database, or to look at the Media Monitor, which includes other statements and responses made to the press. Press Notices goes back to 1998. The Ofsted site includes a list of press notices, by date, going back to 2000 (not searchable).[11] The QCA site also offers a list of press releases, a What's New section showing latest additions to the site, and online access to their newsletter, *OnQ*.[12]

International sources

For a Europe-wide view of education news, Eurydice: The Information Network on Education in Europe[13] provides access to a regular bulletin, *Education in the news – Europe*, compiled from press and web sources. Other online gateways also offer opportunities to investigate news items in a wider context. The Resource Discovery Network (RDN) *Behind the headlines*[14] section provides links to items within the RDN system which include information relevant to recent headline news reports. It now has a searchable archive. The RDN system includes the *British education index resource catalogue* (BEIRC),[15] the *Social science information gateway* (SOSIG)[16] and other subject gateways for higher education. The National Information Services and Systems (NISS) site has a section called *Common room*,[17] which includes a comprehensive listing of links to news sites, both UK and worldwide, and incorporates both indexes and individual papers and magazines.

Newly published

For those working in higher education, the Zetoc service, from the British Library, provides access to the library's *Electronic table of contents* database,[18] covering 20,000 journals, and also conference papers. Conference papers in education are published in full on the *Education-line* database.[19]

Events

Coming events are also sometimes included in news services. Again, printed sources tend to be at a disadvantage here, in being less current. The *Education Authorities Directory and Annual*[20] includes a section on coming events which covers conferences and schools' competitions and championships. An updated version appears on their website. The *TES* website also includes an extensive *Noticeboard* section,[21] listing conferences, training courses, summer schools, exhibitions, competitions and other events.

References

1. Times Newspapers (weekly), *Times Educational Supplement*. London: Times Newspapers.
2. Times Newspapers (weekly), *Times Higher Education Supplement*. London: Times Newspapers.

3. The Guardian (weekly), *Education Guardian*. London and Manchester: Guardian Newspapers Ltd.
4. Independent News and Media, *The Independent*. London: Independent News and Media plc.
5. BUBL UK, *Newspapers* http://bubl.ac.uk/uk/newspapers.htm
6. BBC News, *Education* http://news.bbc.co.uk/1/hi/education
7. Times Newspapers, *Times Educational Supplement* http://www.tes.co.uk
8. The Guardian, *Education Guardian* http://education.guardian.co.uk
9. *British Education Index* (quarterly). Leeds: Leeds University Press. Also available on CD-ROM and electronically. See http://www.leeds.ac.uk/bei/beiaccess.htm
10. Department for Education and Skills, *News centre* http://www.dfes.gov.uk/pns/newslist.cgi
11. Office for Standards in Education, *Ofsted news* http://www.ofsted.gov.uk/news
12. Qualifications and Curriculum Authority, *QCA news* http://www.qca.org.uk/news
13. Eurydice: The Information Network on Education in Europe http://www.eurydice.org
14. Resource Discovery Network, *RDN Behind the headlines* http://www.rdn.ac.uk/bth
15. British Education Index, *British education index resource catalogue* http://brs.leeds.ac.uk/~beiwww/beirc.htm
16. *Social science information gateway* http://www.sosig.ac.uk
17. National Information Services and Systems, *Common room* http://www.niss.ac.uk/cr
18. Zetoc, *Electronic table of contents from the British Library* http://zetoc.mimas.ac.uk
19. British Education Index, *Education-line* http://www.leeds.ac.uk/educol
20. *The Education Authorities Directory and Annual* (annual). Redhill: School Government Publishing.
21. Times Educational Supplement, *Noticeboard* http://www.tes.co.uk/NQT/noticeboard

9 History of education

Historical questions sound straightforward, but can prove surprisingly difficult to answer. Sources for simple chronological queries are not always obvious, as 'time line' information is usually part of a source that has its main focus elsewhere. Online searches, whether of catalogues or the internet, are difficult to structure as the words 'history' and 'education' are both far too common to give useful results. This is an area where it is particularly useful to know where to start looking.

Chronologies

Perhaps the most common type of factual question asked is the one that simply requires a date for some key development or piece of legislation. Some of the sources referred to in Chapter 5 which give lists of key official publications may be useful here. *Education in the UK: Facts and figures*[1] includes sections on both legislation from 1870 and major reports from 1944; Maclure's *Educational Documents: England and Wales, 1816 to the present day*[2] is intended as a source for historical study. Some online sources also provide chronologies. Michael Warren's *A chronology of state medicine, public health, welfare and related services in Britain, 1066–1999*,[3] although focused on public health, includes key dates for education; the additional information provides an interesting context for the educational developments, but makes the process of finding a particular date more cumbersome. The chronology given on *Key dates in education: Great Britain 1000–1899*[4] is more focused, but very brief, and obviously stops short of the complex developments of the twentieth century.

Definitions

For brief definitions of former education practices or institutions, sources of the encyclopedia or dictionary type may be sufficient. Lawton and Gordon's *Dictionary of Education*,[5] for instance, includes brief but useful definitions for terms such as 'dissenting academy', 'ragged schools', 'monitorial system' and 'object lesson'. A more historically focused source of this sort is the website *Education 1750–1950*,[6] part of the Spartacus Internet Encyclopedia, which gives brief but informative entries under the headings 'educationists', 'politicians and education' and 'educational developments'; and for individual schools and colleges, and major Education Acts.

Histories

For more detailed accounts and assessments of past developments in education, it may be necessary to refer to some standard textbooks. Lawson and Silver's *A Social History of Education in England*,[7] although no longer up to date, is still a useful source covering the period AD 600–1972. More detail on the twentieth century can be found in Gordon, Aldrich and Dean's *Education and Policy in England in the Twentieth Century*,[8] which includes both a chronological account of policy developments up to the end of the 1980s and thematic sections on various issues such as curriculum and types of school. For the most recent developments, Clyde Chitty's *The Education System Transformed*[9] gives a brief survey of developments from 1944 to 1979, and detailed discussion of events in the 1980s and 1990s leading up to the New Labour education agenda. Also covering the last two hundred years in some depth is Brian Simon's series of four books, *Studies in the History of Education*. Starting with *The Two Nations and the Educational Structure, 1780–1870*,[10] he considers education in its social and political context, proceeding through *Education and the Labour Movement, 1870–1920*[11] and *The Politics of Educational Reform, 1920–1940*,[12] to a final volume on *Education and the Social Order, 1940–1990*.[13] For those with a Welsh focus, Gareth Elwyn Jones' *The Education of a Nation*[14] covers a range of topics in the history of education in Wales over the last two hundred years.

Individuals

Another aspect of historical enquiry concerns individual educationists. Brief biographical information can be found online in the encyclopedia already mentioned (*Education 1750–1950*)[6] and in printed sources, such as biographical dictionaries. Useful examples include the two companion volumes by Aldrich and Gordon: *Dictionary of British Educationists*[15] and *Biographical Dictionary of North American and European Educationists*.[16] Both contain entries for influential figures from 1800 onwards, but do not cover those still living. In addition to brief details of their subjects' lives, they include useful lists of their writings and suggestions for further reading.

Sources

Access to further information, and primary sources especially, is another common subject for enquiries. For materials available online, there is one outstanding source: *The history of education and childhood* website[17] provides a set of links to other sites on this subject, intended to overcome the difficulties of searching for history and education. It provides links to other websites, online documents and bibliographies – with brief informative comments on each – and is a model of clarity, but no longer appears to be actively updated. For printed materials, apart from searching library catalogues online, the standard published source is still Higson's *Sources for the History of Education* (1967)[18] and its *Supplement* (1976).[19] These cover the holdings of the institutes and schools of education of the older universities, giving details and locations for works published before 1870, and government publications to 1918. Information on holdings of unpublished source material can be found in *British Archives: A guide to archive resources in the United Kingdom.*[20] An index to collections leads to entries by holding institution giving basic details of contacts, addresses and opening hours.

Most of the sources quoted here have referred primarily to the history of education in England, but the field is of course an international one. This is acknowledged in *The history of education and childhood* website;[17] another useful starting point for an international perspective is the *International Guide for Research in the History of Education*[21] produced by the International Standing Conference for the History of Education. For each country, this includes details of associations and centres, chairs of history of education, centres of documentation (such as libraries and museums) and reference books (including research guides, bibliographies, dictionaries etc.).

References

1. MacKinnon, D. and Statham, J. (1999), *Education in the UK: Facts and figures*, 3rd ed. London: Hodder & Stoughton in association with the Open University.
2. Maclure, S. (1985), *Educational Documents: England and Wales, 1816 to the present day*, 5th ed. London: Methuen.
3. Warren, M. (2000), *A chronology of state medicine, public health, welfare and related services in Britain, 1066–1999*
    http://www.chronology.ndo.co.uk/index.htm
4. Birks, S., *Key dates in education: Great Britain 1000–1899*
    http://net1.netcentral.co.uk/steveb/dates/education.htm
5. Lawton, D. and Gordon, P. (1996), *Dictionary of Education*, 2nd ed. London: Hodder & Stoughton.
6. Simkin, J., *Spartacus Educational: Education. 1750–1950*
    http://www.spartacus.schoolnet.co.uk/education.htm
7. Lawson, J. and Silver, H. (1973), *A Social History of Education in England*. London: Methuen.
8. Gordon, P., Aldrich, R. and Dean, D. (1991), *Education and Policy in England in the Twentieth Century*. London: Woburn Press.

9. Chitty, C. (1999), *The Education System Transformed*, 2nd ed. Tisbury: Baseline Book Company.
10. Simon, B. (1974), *The Two Nations and the Educational Structure, 1780–1870*, 2nd ed. London: Lawrence & Wishart.
11. Simon, B. (1965), *Education and the Labour Movement, 1870–1920*. London: Lawrence & Wishart.
12. Simon, B. (1974), *The Politics of Educational Reform, 1920–1940*. London: Lawrence & Wishart.
13. Simon, B. (1991), *Education and the Social Order, 1940–1990*. London: Lawrence & Wishart.
14. Jones, G.E. (1997), *The Education of a Nation*. Cardiff: University of Wales Press.
15. Aldrich, R. and Gordon, P. (1989), *Dictionary of British Educationists*. London: Woburn Press.
16. Gordon, P. and Aldrich, R. (1997), *Biographical Dictionary of North American and European Educationists*. London: Woburn Press.
17. Philosophy and History of Education Institute (University of Nijmegen, Netherlands), *The history of education and childhood* http://www.socsci.kun.nl/ped/whp/histeduc
18. Higson, C.W.J. (1967), *Sources for the History of Education: A list of material (including school books) contained in the libraries of the institutes and schools of education, together with works from the libraries of the Universities of Nottingham and Reading*. London: Library Association.
19. Higson, C.W.J. (1976), *Supplement to Sources for the History of Education: A list of material added to the libraries of the institutes and schools of education, 1965–1974, together with works from certain university libraries*. London: Library Association.
20. Foster, J. and Sheppard, J. (2002), *British Archives: A guide to archive resources in the United Kingdom*, 5th ed. London: Palgrave.
21. Caspard, P. (1995), *Guide international de la recherche en histoire de l'éducation / International Guide for Research in the History of Education*. Paris/Bern: Institut National de Recherche/Peter Lang. 3rd ed. in preparation, will be available online at http://www.inrp.fr/she/work_savoir_plus.htm

10 *The international perspective*

Key questions:
How does education work in Pakistan? At what age do children start school in Finland? Is there an international school in Crete? How can I find out about studying abroad? How can I find details of teaching jobs abroad?

Thorough coverage of international sources would require far more space than we have available in this book. Most chapters could include an international section alongside resources for the UK, and where appropriate we have offered some starting points for wider enquiry. This section aims to bring together some of the most frequently asked questions with an obvious international focus, and to provide a few useful pointers in a very large field.

Education systems

One obvious need is for descriptive information on the education systems of other countries. This is provided in a simple, standardised format in the *International Encyclopedia of Education*, edited by Husén and Postlethwaite.[1] The printed version of the encyclopedia (12 volumes, arranged in the normal alphabetical format) appeared in its second edition in 1994. More detailed information on higher education is provided in the *Encyclopedia of Higher Education*,[2] from the same publisher. The printed version, which came out in 1992, covers national systems of higher education in its first volume, and includes articles on other aspects and issues in the remaining three volumes. *Education: The complete encyclopedia*[3] includes updated versions of both these publications on one CD-ROM. As well as being more recent, issued in 1998, it has the advantage of electronic searching capabilities.

For more detailed information on Europe, Eurydice: The Information Network for Education in Europe gives access to *Eurybase*,[4] a database of information on education systems. Eurydice also offers a range of publications covering such issues as key competencies, school hours, information and communication technology (ICT) and initial teacher education requirements across Europe. A useful source for higher education in Europe is *A Guide to Higher Education Systems and Qualifications in the EU and EEA Countries*,[5] which provides a chapter on each country, describing the system of higher education and the types of qualifications awarded; it is also available online.[6]

Schools and colleges

More specific enquiries are often directed at finding information about particular institutions, either schools or colleges. Information about schools within the state system of other countries is not readily available but, for those contemplating living abroad, there are a number of useful directories of international schools. These typically offer a curriculum on either the British or American model, taught through the medium of English, to pupils of many nationalities. Robert Findlay's *International Education Handbook*[7] includes a useful introductory section on understanding international education and chapters on international education issues, as well as a directory of schools; *The ISS Directory of Overseas Schools*[8] is a straightforward directory, produced in the US; *The John Catt Guide to International Schools*[9] is another in the series of directories from this publisher, and like their UK guides *(Which School?* etc.), can also be accessed via the *Schoolsearch* website.[10]

Probably the most comprehensive of these directories is *The International Schools Directory*[11] published by the European Council for International Schools (ECIS). As well as quite substantial entries for individual schools, some of which are also accredited by ECIS, it includes lists of associate members (mostly colleges and universities), affiliate members (offering specialist services such as summer camps) and supporting members (educational suppliers). ECIS also publish *The ECIS Higher Education Directory*,[12] giving fuller details of its college and university members, mostly British and American universities which are actively recruiting students from overseas. All this information, and more, is available on the excellent ECIS website.[13] This covers the full range of ECIS activities including, as well as the directories, professional development opportunities such as conferences, and information services such as the provision of bibliographies and current awareness services.

Working and studying abroad

Another useful section on the ECIS website[13] covers recruitment services, and would make a good starting point for those seeking information on finding employment overseas as a teacher. ECIS organises recruitment fairs, maintains a register of job seekers and provides a listing of vacancies in member schools. The British Council also work in this field. Their website[14] includes information for teachers on a wide variety of training opportunities, jobs, visits and exchanges – lasting up to a year – in Europe, the United States and China. Other sections cover programmes for schools and colleges (including partnership and exchange schemes with schools abroad) and also a section on opportunities specifically for headteachers.

Enquiries about studying abroad are also common. Information about both studying and working in higher education is available from the Association of Commonwealth Universities (ACU) website.[15] For students, it provides both general information and a searchable directory of courses. For staff, there is a vacancies section as well as details of conferences and other publications. Best known of the ACU's publications is the *Commonwealth Universities Yearbook*,[16] a comprehensive directory of universities in Commonwealth countries, including not only location and address but also names of all senior academic staff members for each university. It is published annually. Extending coverage even wider is *The World of Learning*,[17] a comprehensive directory which covers learned societies, research institutes, libraries and archives, and museums and art galleries, as well as higher education. Similar directories, providing varying amounts of detail, exist for other countries and regions, notably the United States. For example, *Peterson's*

Register of Higher Education[18] is a directory of institutions and their senior staff; *Barron's Profiles of American Colleges*[19] gives fuller information for intending students. The Peterson's website[20] includes comprehensive listings of courses and colleges, as well as other aspects of education and careers information.

For more general information, rather than simply names and addresses, a number of handbooks offer advice and guidance to students looking for opportunities to study abroad. The Department for Education and Skills (DfES) produce *The European choice: a guide to opportunities for higher education in Europe*.[21] This gives some general information, including sources of financial support, and a directory of countries giving a brief outline of the higher education system and opportunities, and sources of further information. A series of country handbooks from On Course Publications includes *Study in France Handbook*[22] and *Study in Spain Handbook*.[23] These provide useful background information on living and studying in the country concerned, and details of short courses. Language schools are also covered, but universities have only a brief listing.

The British Council website is also a useful starting point for more information, especially on Europe. It includes a comprehensive set of links to other sites concerning Europe from its *Education and training* pages.[14] Parallel organisations in other countries, such as the Goethe Institute[24] and the Institut Français,[25] provide further information about their home countries.

References

1. Husén, T. and Postlethwaite, T.N. eds (1994), *International Encyclopedia of Education: Research and studies*, 2nd ed. Oxford: Pergamon.
2. Clark, B.R. and Neave, G. eds (1992), *Encyclopedia of Higher Education*. Oxford: Pergamon.
3. Husén, T. (1998), *Education: The complete encyclopedia* (CD-ROM). Oxford: Pergamon.
4. Eurydice, *Eurybase 2001 The information database on education systems in Europe* http://www.eurydice.org
5. Commission of the European Communities. Directorate-General for Education Training and Youth (1998), *A Guide to Higher Education*

Systems and Qualifications in the EU and EEA Countries, 2nd ed. Luxembourg: Office for Official Publications of the European Community.

6. The European Commission. Socrates-Erasmus, *A guide to higher education systems and qualifications in the EU and EEA countries* http://europa.eu.int/comm/education/socrates/erasmus/guide
7. Findlay, R. (1997), *International Education Handbook*. London: Kogan Page in association with Educational Relocation Association.
8. International Schools Services (annual), *The ISS Directory of Overseas Schools: The comprehensive guide to K-12 American and international schools worldwide*. Princeton, NJ: ISS.
9. Bingham, D. ed. (annual), *The John Catt Guide to International Schools*. Saxmundham: John Catt Educational.
10. John Catt Educational, *John Catt's schoolsearch* http://www.schoolsearch.co.uk
11. European Council of International Schools (annual), *The International Schools Directory*. Petersfield: John Catt Educational for the European Council of International Schools.
12. European Council of International Schools (annual), *The ECIS Higher Education Directory: Institutions in membership of the European Council of International Schools*. London: Specialist Publishing Services for ECIS.
13. European Council for International Schools http://www.ecis.org
14. British Council, *Education and training* http://www.britishcouncil.org/education/index.htm
15. Association of Commonwealth Universities http://www.acu.ac.uk
16. Association of Commonwealth Universities (annual), *Commonwealth Universities Yearbook: A directory to the universities of the Commonwealth and the handbook of their Association*. London: ACU.
17. *The World of Learning* (annual). London: Europa.
18. *Peterson's Register of Higher Education* (1997). Princeton, NJ: Peterson's Guides.
19. *Barron's Profiles of American Colleges* (1997), 22nd ed. New York: Barron's Educational Series.
20. Peterson's *Colleges and universities* http://www.petersons.com/ugchannel
21. Department for Education and Skills, National Academic Recognition Information Centre for the United Kingdom, and ECCTIS, *The European*

choice: a guide for higher education opportunities in Europe
http://www.eurochoice.org.uk

22. Tucker, L. (1999), *Study in France Handbook*. London: On Course Publications.

23. Goulden, S. (1999), *Study in Spain Handbook*. London: On Course Publications.

24. Goethe Institute London http://www.goethe.de/gr/lon/enindex.htm

25. Institut Français http://www.institut-francais.org.uk

Bibliography

Printed sources

A complete list of printed resources referred to in the text.

Aldrich, R. and Gordon, P. (1989), *Dictionary of British Educationists*. London: Woburn Press.

Association of Commonwealth Universities (annual), *Commonwealth Universities Yearbook: A directory to the universities of the Commonwealth and the handbook of their Association*. London: ACU.

Association of National Specialist Colleges (2001), *Directory 2001 and 2002*. Association of National Specialist Colleges.

Barron's Profiles of American Colleges (1997), 22nd ed. New York: Barron's Educational Series.

Bingham, D. ed. (annual), *The John Catt Guide to International Schools*. Saxmundham: John Catt Educational.

Boehm, K. ed. (annual), *The Guide to Independent Schools*. Richmond: Trotman.

Booth, T. and Ainscow, M. (2002), *Index for Inclusion: Developing learning and participation in schools*, revised ed. Bristol: Centre for Studies on Inclusive Education, University of the West of England.

British Council (1996/8), *Access to UK Higher Education: A guide for international students*. London: HMSO.

British Council (1996), *International Guide to Qualifications in Education*, 4th ed. London: British Council, National Academic Recognition Information Centre for the United Kingdom.

British Education Index (quarterly). Leeds: Leeds University Press.

British Qualifications: A complete guide to educational, technical, professional and academic qualifications in Britain (annual). London: Kogan Page.

British Vocational Qualifications: A directory of vocational qualifications available in the UK (annual), London: Kogan Page.

Caspard, P. (1995), *Guide international de la recherche en histoire de l'éducation/International Guide for Research in the History of Education.* Paris/Bern: Institut National de Recherche/Peter Lang. 3rd ed. in preparation, will be available online at http://www.inrp.fr/she/work_savoir_plus.htm

Chartered Institute of Public Finance and Accountancy. Statistical Information Service (annual), *Education Statistics: Actuals.* London: CIPFA.

Chartered Institute of Public Finance and Accountancy. Statistical Information Service (annual), *Education Statistics: Estimates.* London: CIPFA.

Chitty, C. (1999), *The Education System Transformed*, 2nd ed. Tisbury: Baseline Book Company.

Clare, J. ed. (1998), *The Daily Telegraph Schools Guide 1998–99: The definitive guide to the best independent and state schools.* London: Robinson.

Clark, B.R. and Neave, G. eds (1992), *Encyclopedia of Higher Education.* Oxford: Pergamon.

Commission of the European Communities. Directorate-General for Education Training and Youth (1998), *A Guide to Higher Education Systems and Qualifications in the EU and EEA Countries*, 2nd ed. Luxembourg: Office for Official Publications of the European Community.

Commission of the European Communities, Eurydice, and Commission of the European Communities Statistical Office (2000), *Key Data on Education in Europe.* Luxembourg: European Commission.

The Complete Degree Course Offers: The comprehensive guide on entry to universities and colleges (annual). Richmond: Trotman.

Croner's Manual for Heads of Science (1991–). Kingston upon Thames: Croner.

Department for Education and Employment (1999), *The National Curriculum for England. Handbook for primary teachers in England: key stages 1 and 2.* London: The Stationery Office for DfEE and QCA.

Department for Education and Employment (1999), *The National Curriculum for England. Handbook for secondary teachers in England: key stages 3 and 4.* London: The Stationery Office for DfEE and QCA.

Department for Education and Employment. Standards and Effectiveness Unit (1999), *The National Numeracy Strategy. Framework for teaching mathematics, from reception to year 6.* London: DfEE.

Department for Education and Skills (annual), *Education and Training Statistics for the United Kingdom.* London: The Stationery Office.

Department for Education and Skills (2001), *National Literacy Strategy: Framework for teaching*, 3rd ed. London: DfES.

Department for Education and Skills (irregular), *Public Examinations GCSE/ GNVQ and GCE/AGNVQ in England.* London: The Stationery Office.

Department for Education and Skills (2001), *Special Educational Needs Code of Practice.* Annesley: DfES Publications.

Department for Education and Skills (irregular), *Statistics of Education: School workforce in England.* London: The Stationery Office.

Department for Education and Skills (irregular), *Statistics of Education: Schools in England.* London: The Stationery Office.

Department for Education and Skills (irregular), *Student Support England and Wales.* London: The Stationery Office.

Directory of Vocational and Further Education (annual). London: Pitman.

Education and the Law (1989–). Harlow: Longman.

The Education Authorities Directory and Annual (annual). Redhill: School Government Publishing.

Education Law Journal (2000–). Bristol: Jordan Publishing.

Education Law Reports (1994–). Bristol: Jordan Publishing.

Education Year Book (annual). London: Longman for the Association of Education Committees.

Education, Public Law and the Individual (1996–). Bognor Regis: John Wiley & Sons.

European Council of International Schools (annual), *The ECIS Higher Education Directory: Institutions in membership of the European Council of International Schools.* London: Specialist Publishing Services for ECIS.

European Council of International Schools (annual), *The International Schools Directory.* Petersfield: John Catt Educational for the European Council of International Schools.

Eurydice European Unit (1999), *European Glossary on Education. Vol. 1: Examinations, qualifications and titles.* Brussels: Eurydice European Unit.

Farrell, M., Kerry, T. and Kerry, C. (1995), *Blackwell Handbook of Education.* Oxford: Blackwell.

Findlay, R. (1998), *Choose the Right Primary School: A guide to primary schools in England, Scotland and Wales.* London: The Stationery Office.

Findlay, R. (1998), *Choose the Right Secondary School: A guide to secondary schools in England, Scotland and Wales*. London: The Stationery Office.

Findlay, R. (1997), *International Education Handbook*. London: Kogan Page in association with Educational Relocation Association.

Ford, J., Hughes, M. and Ruebain, D. (1999), *Education Law and Practice*. London: Legal Action Group.

Foster, J. and Sheppard, J. (2002), *British Archives: A guide to archive resources in the United Kingdom*, 5th ed. London: Palgrave.

Frederickson, N. and Cline, T. (2002), *Special Educational Needs, Inclusion and Diversity: A textbook*. Buckingham: Open University Press.

Gabbitas Educational Consultants (2000), *The Gabbitas Guide to Schools for Special Needs*, 6th ed. London: Kogan Page.

Gabbitas Educational Consultants (annual), *The Independent Schools Guide*. London: Kogan Page.

Gabbitas Truman & Thring Educational Trust (annual), *Which School?* Saxmundham: John Catt.

Gabbitas Truman & Thring Educational Trust (annual), *Which school? at Sixteen*. Saxmundham: John Catt.

Gabbitas Truman & Thring Educational Trust (annual), *Which School? for Special Needs: A guide to independent and non-maintained schools*. Saxmundham: John Catt.

Gearon, L. (2002), *Education in the United Kingdom: Structures and organisation*. London: David Fulton.

Gold, R. and Szemerenyi, S. (annual), *Running a School: Legal duties and responsibilities*. Bristol: Jordan Publishing.

Gordon, P. and Aldrich, R. (1997), *Biographical Dictionary of North American and European Educationists*. London: Woburn Press.

Gordon, P., Aldrich, R. and Dean, D. (1991), *Education and Policy in England in the Twentieth Century*. London: Woburn Press.

Goulden, S. (1999), *Study in Spain Handbook*. London: On Course Publications.

Grant, C.A. and Ladson-Billings, G. eds (1997), *Dictionary of Multicultural Education*. Phoenix, Ariz.: Oryx Press.

The Guardian (weekly), *Education Guardian*. London and Manchester: Guardian Newspapers Ltd.

Higher Education Careers Services Unit (2000), *Prospects Postgraduate*

Directory: The official guide, with over 4,500 UK courses and research opportunities. Manchester: CSU.

Higher Education Statistics Agency (annual), *First Destinations of Students Leaving Higher Education Institutions*. Cheltenham: HESA.

Higher Education Statistics Agency (annual), *Higher Education Management Statistics. Sector level*. Cheltenham: HESA.

Higher Education Statistics Agency (annual), *Higher Education Statistics for the United Kingdom*. Cheltenham: HESA.

Higher Education Statistics Agency (annual), *Resources of Higher Education Institutions*. Cheltenham: HESA.

Higher Education Statistics Agency (annual), *Students in Higher Education Institutions*. Cheltenham: HESA.

Higson, C.W.J. (1967), *Sources for the History of Education: A list of material (including school books) contained in the libraries of the institutes and schools of education, together with works from the libraries of the Universities of Nottingham and Reading*. London: Library Association.

Higson, C.W.J. (1976), *Supplement to Sources for the History of Education: A list of material added to the libraries of the institutes and schools of education, 1965-1974, together with works from certain university libraries*. London: Library Association.

Holt, G., Boyd, S., Dickinson, B., Loose, J. and O'Donnell, S. (1999), *Education in England, Wales and Northern Ireland: A guide to the system*, new ed. Slough: National Foundation for Educational Research.

Howarth, S.B. (1984–), *The Head's Legal Guide*. New Malden: Croner.

Husén, T. and Postlethwaite, T.N. eds (1994), *International Encyclopedia of Education: Research and studies*, 2nd ed. Oxford: Pergamon; also available on CD-ROM: Husén, T. (1998), *Education: The complete encyclopedia*. Oxford: Pergamon.

Hyams, O. (1998), *Law of Education*. London: Sweet & Maxwell.

Independent News and Media, *The Independent*. London: Independent News and Media plc.

International Association of Universities (biennial), *International Handbook of Universities: And other institutions of higher education*. London: Macmillan.

International Schools Services (annual), *The ISS Directory of Overseas Schools: The comprehensive guide to K-12 American and international schools worldwide*. Princeton, NJ: ISS.

Jones, G.E. (1997), *The Education of a Nation*. Cardiff: University of Wales Press.

Lawson, J. and Silver, H. (1973), *A Social History of Education in England*. London: Methuen.

Lawton, D. and Gordon, P. (1996), *Dictionary of Education*, 2nd ed. London: Hodder & Stoughton.

Learning and Skills Council (annual), *Staff Statistics*. London: LSC.

Learning and Skills Council (annual), *Student Statistics*. London: LSC.

Learning and Skills Council (annual), *Summary Statistics for Further Education Institutions*. London: LSC.

Liell, P., Saunders, J.B., and Taylor, G. eds (1984–), *The Law of Education*, 9th ed. London: Butterworths.

Lloyd, J.G. (1999), *How Exams Really Work: The Cassell guide to GCSEs, AS and A Levels*. London: Cassell.

Lowe, J. (1998), *The Home Education Handbook: A practical guide to home education*. Welwyn Garden City: Home Education Advisory Service.

MacKinnon, D. and Statham, J. (1999), *Education in the UK: Facts and figures*, 3rd ed. London: Hodder & Stoughton in association with the Open University.

Maclure, S. (1985), *Educational Documents: England and Wales, 1816 to the present day*, 5th ed. London: Methuen.

Macpherson of Cluny, Sir William (chairman) (1999), *The Stephen Lawrence Inquiry (report of an inquiry)*. London: The Stationery Office.

McCaffrey, K. (annual), *The Push Guide to Which University*. London: The Stationery Office.

National Assembly for Wales (annual), *Schools in Wales: Examination performance*. Cardiff: National Assembly for Wales.

National Assembly for Wales (annual), *Schools in Wales: General statistics*. Cardiff: National Assembly for Wales.

National Association for Special Educational Needs (1985–), *British Journal of Special Education*. Tamworth: NASEN.

National Association for Special Educational Needs (1986–), *Support for Learning*. Oxford: Blackwell.

Office for National Statistics (irregular), *Guide to Official Statistics*. London: The Stationery Office.

Office for National Statistics (annual), *Regional Trends*. London: National Statistics.

Office for National Statistics (annual), *Social Trends*. London: National Statistics.

Organisation for Economic Co-operation and Development (annual), *Education at a Glance: OECD indicators*. London: The Stationery Office.

Peterson's Register of Higher Education (1997). Princeton, NJ: Peterson's Guides.

Postlethwaite, T.N. ed. (1995), *International Encyclopedia of National Systems of Education*, 2nd ed. Oxford: Elsevier.

The Primary Education Directory (annual). Redhill: School Government Publishing Company.

School Governor's Manual (1992–). Kingston upon Thames: Croner.

Simon, B. (1965), *Education and the Labour Movement, 1870–1920*. London: Lawrence & Wishart.

Simon, B. (1991), *Education and the Social Order, 1940–1990*. London: Lawrence & Wishart.

Simon, B. (1974), *The Politics of Educational Reform, 1920–1940*. London: Lawrence & Wishart.

Simon, B. (1974), *The Two Nations and the Educational Structure, 1780–1870*, 2nd ed. London: Lawrence & Wishart.

Smeaton, R.F. (1999), *Researching Education: Reference tools and networks*. London: Librarians of Institutes and Schools of Education.

The Special Education Directory (annual). Redhill: School Government Publishing Company.

Times Newspapers (weekly), *Times Educational Supplement*. London: Times Newspapers.

Times Newspapers (weekly), *Times Higher Education supplement*. London: Times Newspapers.

Tucker, L. (1999), *Study in France Handbook*. London: On Course Publications.

United Nations Educational Scientific and Cultural Organisation, *Unesco Statistical Yearbook*. Paris: Unesco Publishing and Bernan Press. Last published 1999.

Universities and Colleges Admissions Service for the UK (annual), *University and College Entrance: The official guide* (sometimes entitled *The big guide*). Cheltenham: UCAS.

University of Bristol Graduate School of Education (2002), *Teachers' Legal*

Liabilities and Responsibilities: The Bristol guide, revised and extended ed. Bristol: University of Bristol Graduate School of Education.
Whitaker's Almanack (annual). London: The Stationery Office.
The World of Learning (annual). London: Europa.

Websites

In the case of large websites, only the home page is listed here. For specific URLs within those sites more detail is provided within appropriate chapters.

ACE: Advisory Centre for Education http://www.ace-ed.org.uk
Allfie: Alliance for Inclusive Education http://www.allfie.org.uk
Assessment and Qualifications Alliance http://www.aqa.org.uk
Association of Commonwealth Universities http://www.acu.ac.uk
Basic Skills Agency http://www.basic-skills.co.uk
BBC News, *Education* http://news.bbc.co.uk/1/hi/education
Birks, S., *Key dates in education: Great Britain 1000–1899*
    http://net1.netcentral.co.uk/steveb/dates/education.htm
British Council, *Education and training* http://www.britishcouncil.org/
    education/index.htm
British Council, *Education UK* http://www.educationuk.org
British Education Index http://www.leeds.ac.uk/bei/beiaccess.htm
British Education Index, *British education index resource catalogue*
    http://brs.leeds.ac.uk/~beiwww/beirc.htm
British Education Index, *Education-line* http://www.leeds.ac.uk/educol
British Educational Communications and Technology Agency
    http://www.becta.org.uk
BUBL UK http://bubl.ac.uk/uk
Centre for Studies on Inclusive Education http://inclusion.uwe.ac.uk
Commission for Racial Equality http://www.cre.gov.uk
Department for Education and Skills http://www.dfes.gov.uk
Department for Education and Skills, *Adult learners' gateway*
    http://www.dfes.gov.uk/adultlearners
Department for Education and Skills, *Special educational needs code of
    practice* http://www.dfes.gov.uk/sen/viewDocument.cfm?dID=260

Department for Education and Skills, *The Standards site*
http://www.standards.dfes.gov.uk
Department for Education and Skills, *Statistics*
http://www.dfes.gov.uk/statistics
Department for Education and Skills, *Teachernet* http://www.teachernet.gov.uk
Department for Education and Skills, National Academic Recognition Information Centre for the United Kingdom, and ECCTIS, *The European choice: a guide for higher education opportunities in Europe*
http://www.eurochoice.org.uk
Department for Work and Pensions, *Disability Discrimination Act*
http://www.disability.gov.uk/dda
Edexcel http://www.edexcel.org.uk
Estyn: Her Majesty's Inspectorate for Education and Training in Wales
http://www.estyn.gov.uk
European Centre for the Development of Vocational Training
http://www.cedefop.gr
The European Commission. Socrates-Erasmus, *A guide to higher education systems and qualifications in the EU and EEA countries* http://europa.eu.int/comm/education/socrates/erasmus/guide
European Council of International Schools http://www.ecis.org
Eurydice: The Information Network on Education in Europe
http://www.eurydice.org
Examinations Appeals Board http://www.theeab.org.uk
Goethe Institute London http://www.goethe.de/gr/lon/enindex.htm
The Guardian, *Education Guardian* http://education.guardian.co.uk
Her Majesty's Stationery Office http://www.hmso.gov.uk
Higher Education Funding Council for England http://www.hefce.ac.uk
Higher Education Funding Council for Wales http://www.wfc.ac.uk/hefcw
Higher Education Statistics Agency http://www.hesa.ac.uk
Home Education Advisory Service http://www.heas.org.uk
Home Office, *Race equality and diversity* http://www.homeoffice.gov.uk/new_indexs/index_racial-equality.htm
Home Office, *Race Relations (Amendment) Act 2000 and the EC Article 13 Race Directive*
http://www.homeoffice.gov.uk/raceact/welcome.htm
Hutchins, J. (1995), *Acronyms and initialisms in education: a handlist*
http://www.educ.cam.ac.uk/lise/acronyms.doc

Independent Schools of the British Isles, *ISBI the database*
http://www.earl.org.uk/isbi
Institut Français http://www.institut-francais.org.uk
Institute of Education University of London, *Information services*
http://www.ioe.ac.uk/infoserv
John Catt Educational, *John Catt's schoolsearch*
http://www.schoolsearch.co.uk
Joint Council for General Qualifications http://www.jcgq.org.uk
Learning and Skills Council http://www.lsc.gov.uk
Learning and Teaching Scotland http://www.ltscotland.com
Macpherson of Cluny, Sir William (chairman), *The Stephen Lawrence inquiry
(report of an inquiry)* http://www.archive.official-documents.co.uk/
document/cm42/4262/4262.htm
National Academic Recognition Information Centre for the United Kingdom,
UK NARIC http://www.naric.org.uk
National Assembly for Wales, *Learning Wales*
http://www.learning.wales.gov.uk
National Association for Special Educational Needs (2001–), *Journal of
research in special educational needs* http://www.nasen.uk.com/ejournal
National Association for Special Educational Needs http://www.nasen.org.uk
National Grid for Learning http://www.ngfl.gov.uk
National Information Services and Systems http://www.niss.ac.uk
National Institute of Adult Continuing Education http://www.niace.org.uk
National Statistics, *Online* http://www.statistics.gov.uk
Northern Ireland Council for the Curriculum, Examinations and Assessment
http://www.ccea.org.uk
Office for Standards in Education http://www.ofsted.gov.uk
Organisation for Economic Co-operation and Development
http://www.oecd.org
Oxford, Cambridge and RSA Examinations http://www.ocr.org.uk
Peterson's *Colleges and universities* http://www.petersons.com/ugchannel
Philosophy and History of Education Institute (University of Nijmegen,
Netherlands), *The history of education and childhood*
http://www.socsci.kun.nl/ped/whp/histeduc
Qualifications and Curriculum Authority, *National Curriculum online*
http://www.nc.uk.net
Qualifications and Curriculum Authority http://www.qca.org.uk

Qualifications Curriculum and Assessment Authority for Wales
http://www.accac.org.uk
Quality Assurance Agency for Higher Education http://www.qaa.ac.uk
Resource Discovery Network, *RDN Behind the headlines*
http://www.rdn.ac.uk/bth
Scottish Executive, *Executive online* http://www.scotland.gov.uk
Scottish Higher Education Funding Council http://www.shefc.ac.uk
Scottish Qualifications Authority http://www.sqa.org.uk
Simkin, J., *Spartacus Educational: Education 1750–1950*
http://www.spartacus.schoolnet.co.uk/education.htm
Skill: National Bureau for Students with Disabilities http://www.skill.org.uk
Social science information gateway http://www.sosig.ac.uk
Special Educational Needs Joint Initiative for Training
http://www.ioe.ac.uk/senjit
The Stationery Office, *Official documents* http://www.official-documents.co.uk
Statistical Office of the European Communities, *Eurostat* http://europa.eu.int/
comm/eurostat
Teacher Training Agency http://www.canteach.gov.uk
TechDis http://www.techdis.ac.uk
Times Newspapers, *Times Educational Supplement* http://www.tes.co.uk
The United Kingdom Parliament http://www.parliament.uk
United Nations Educational Scientific and Cultural Organisation
http://www.unesco.org
Universities and Colleges Admissions Service for the UK, *UCAS directory
online* http://www.ucas.ac.uk
University for Industry, *Learndirect* http://www.learndirect.co.uk
Warren, M. (2000), *A chronology of state medicine, public health, welfare
and related services in Britain, 1066–1999*
http://www.chronology.ndo.co.uk/index.htm
Welsh Joint Education Committee http://www.wjec.co.uk
Zetoc, *Electronic table of contents from the British Library*
http://zetoc.mimas.ac.uk